Around
Tenbury Wells

IN OLD PHOTOGRAPHS

Around Tenbury Wells

IN OLD PHOTOGRAPHS

DAVID GREEN

Alan Sutton Publishing Limited
Phoenix Mill · Far Thrupp · Stroud
Gloucestershire

First Published 1994

Cover photograph: The Royal Oak, Market
Street, at the end of the last century.

British Library Cataloguing in Publication Data.
A catalogue record for this book is available from
the British Library.

ISBN 0-7509-0834-3

Typeset in 9/10 Sabon.
Typesetting and origination by
Alan Sutton Publishing Limited.
Printed in Great Britain by
Ebenezer Baylis, Worcester.

Contents

TENBURY

Heare hills doo lift their heads aloft
From whence sweet springs doo flowe,
Whose moistur good doth firtil make
The valleis couchte belowe.
Heare goodly orchards planted are
In fruite which doo abounde;
Thine ey wolde make thine hart rejoyce
To see so pleasant ground.

These lines are taken from the Worcestershire Tapestry Map, dating from the reign of Queen Elizabeth I, in the Victoria and Albert Museum, London.

Introduction

Whether or not Queen Victoria actually said that Tenbury Wells was 'her little town in the orchard' is a moot point. If she did, then it was an appropriately endearing remark to make. If she didn't, then many a writer over the years has unashamedly put words into the royal mouth in the certain knowledge that Her Majesty would indeed have found Tenbury and its orchards an especially agreeable corner of her vast realm.

The orchards have now sadly diminished in extent, as have the once widespread hopyards (not 'hopfields' as in other parts of England) which formerly characterized the Tenbury countryside. But agriculture still predominates, and fortunately there are still enough surviving orchards and hopyards to remind us of the vital role they once played in the economy of the silvan valley of the River Teme.

Tenbury, too, has changed over the years, yet in a far less dramatic way than some other old English market towns. It has successfully shrugged off many of the brasher manifestations of twentieth-century town planning, and its intrinsic character, as well as much of its visual charm, have survived largely intact. A handful of modern housing developments, an impressive new indoor swimming pool and a boldly designed public library may be inevitable concessions to contemporary architectural fashions, but there is no place here for the vast supermarket or the ubiquitous multi-storey car-park.

Tenbury values its architectural heritage, and even if it mourns the loss of a few memorable landmarks, the streets are still graced by many handsome buildings. Bizarre rather than handsome, however, are the extraordinary remains of Tenbury's erstwhile Pump Room by the side of the little Kyre Brook, a quaint reminder of the town's brief heyday as a spa following the discovery of

An engraving of Tenbury seen across the Teme, published by the eighteenth-century county historian Dr Treadway Nash in his celebrated *History of Worcestershire*.

a mineral spring in the last century. These semi-derelict metal-clad buildings, dominated by the skeletal remains of a Chinese-style pagoda, were originally intended to appeal to the arthritic and rheumatic members of the 'middling and lower classes' who, it was presumed, may have felt a little out of place in more salubrious spa towns like Droitwich, Cheltenham, Leamington or Malvern. Unfortunately, most of the 'middling and lower classes' must have resorted to other means for treating their aches and pains, for although the Pump Room did dispense its therapeutic remedies for a number of years, its limited patronage spelt doom for its future, and it ceased operating in 1939.

The partly medieval bridge over the Teme, guarded on the Worcestershire bank by the Bridge Hotel, and on the Shropshire bank by the Swan Hotel, is another noteworthy feature of the townscape. With a curious bend in it midstream, which it acquired when it was extended in the seventeenth century, it has witnessed in its long life the many disastrous occasions when the capricious waters of the Teme have burst their banks and inundated not only the surrounding countryside, but large areas of the town itself.

A prominent reminder of the town's ancient origins lies not far from the bridge. This is a strange conical mound known as the Castle Tump, which, over the years, has generated many a local legend. Some say it was a Bronze Age burial mound, others that it was the base of a Norman wooden keep. Both explanations seem a little more likely than the theory that it marks the last resting place of Caractacus who was killed fighting the Roman invaders in AD 100. But whatever the true origin of this mysterious grassy hillock, the local people continue to hold it in affectionate regard, and the visitors take a quizzical glance at it as they pass by.

Although, as a market town, Tenbury is only of modest size, it nevertheless serves an unusually wide surrounding rural area, and it has always played a significant role in the commercial life of the region. After all, the town's regular markets, which are still a traditional feature of local life, owe their origin to as long ago as the thirteenth century when Henry III granted Tenbury a special charter.

Long gone now are the days when the town's traders and the fruit and hop growers relied for transport on horse-drawn wagons and the canal. Long gone too is the railway which served the town from the 1860s until Dr Beeching summarily axed it a century later. Today the course of the old line can still be traced, in part at least, but the site of Tenbury's former railway station is now ignominiously submerged beneath a bustling industrial estate.

The motor car and the lorry now reign supreme. Where once the patient draught horses were tethered at the kerbside, yellow lines now pronounce their admonitory warning to all who use the town's thoroughfares. The social and economic pressures brought about by so-called progress over the years, have made their mark on Tenbury no less convincingly than anywhere else.

Yes, there has certainly been change, perhaps more so in the last hundred years than at any other period in the town's history, as the pictures in the following pages evocatively illustrate. But Tenbury, on the whole, has taken it all in its stride, intent upon preserving its innate character and independence, and justly proud of its reputation as one of the fairest little towns in Worcestershire.

And all the while the restless waters of the Teme flow by on their journey to the Severn and the sea, as they have since time immemorial.

Tenbury Townscape

Unlike many of England's market towns, Tenbury Wells has not been unduly spoilt by obtrusive and unsympathetic town-centre development on the grand scale. The main streets may not have entirely escaped unaltered, and a few of the old buildings have indeed given way to modern replacements, while others have undergone various degrees of cosmetic surgery. But on the whole the architectural character of the town has managed to survive, and the pictures in the following pages eloquently demonstrate just how much – but occasionally, how little – Tenbury has changed in the last hundred years or so.

An 1892 view of the bridge over the River Teme looking north, with the Swan Hotel in the background. The three northern arches are medieval, the others being added in the seventeenth century when the bridge was extended after flood damage and a change in the river's course.

Another 1892 photograph of the bridge. Following the extension of the bridge in the seventeenth century, further severe flood damage occurred, and in 1815 the structure was strengthened and widened by the famous Scottish engineer, Thomas Telford.

Taken in the latter years of the last century, this picture shows the arch of the bridge which marks the county boundary. The lady stands in Shropshire and the man in Worcestershire.

By 1904, following yet more flood damage, the bridge was again in need of urgent restoration. Four years later it was to undergo extensive repair work.

Preparations for the major repairs to the bridge which took place in 1908. Scaffolding is being erected to support the arches.

The restoration of the bridge in progress, 1908. The curious bend in the middle was acquired when the original medieval bridge was extended in the seventeenth century.

The impressive façade of the Swan Hotel overlooks the bridge on the Shropshire side. In this scene from the gracious days of Edwardian England, cars await guests emerging from the main entrance.

With the 1908 bridge repairs completed, engineers test the strength of one of the arches. Hauled by a steam traction engine, a wagon loaded with several tons of stone stops on the roadway while surveyors measure any signs of movement below.

The restored bridge in 1908, complete with new railings, attracts the attention of local sightseers. The bend in the middle is clearly visible in this picture.

Near the northern end of the bridge stands Tenbury Hospital, seen here in the early years of the century. Originally a large house, it was converted to a hospital in Victorian times.

Guarding the southern end of the bridge is the former workhouse where inmates could qualify for a night's lodging by breaking stones. Remodelled in 1937, the building served as offices for the old Tenbury Rural District Council before becoming the headquarters of Tenbury Town Council.

Teme Street from the bridge around the turn of the century. When the 1908 restoration of the bridge took place, these railings were replaced by the more ornate style seen in the picture below.

The same view of Teme Street after the bridge was repaired. The Bridge Hotel in the right foreground also seems to have received a facelift.

A late-Victorian view of Teme Street. The premises of Hardeman's, the cider merchants, on the left, have now been replaced by a row of modern shops.

Another view of Teme Street around the turn of the century. No modern driver in his right mind would park his car in the fashion chosen by the owner of the splendid vehicle seen here.

Teme Street looking north around 1900. The building with the prominent first-floor bow window on the right was – and still is – the post office. Although the horse-drawn vehicle still appears to predominate, the motor car was evidently becoming popular, judging by the garage sign on the left.

Another photograph of Teme Street taken around the same time as the one above. The building partly visible on the extreme right, formerly a pharmacy and now the Country Restaurant, was once the home of Dr Henry Hill Hickman, the nineteenth-century pioneer in anaesthesia. The adjacent shops have now given way to a modern library and entrance to a car-park.

In 1897 the flags were out in Teme Street for Queen Victoria's Diamond Jubilee. The building in the far distance is The Court, former home of the influential Godson family. It was demolished in the 1960s. In the left foreground is the former police station, now a doctors' surgery.

More flags and bunting in honour of Queen Victoria's Diamond Jubilee. This is the view down Teme Street from its junction with Market Street.

Horse-drawn carts make their leisurely way along Teme Street at the end of the last century. Many of the buildings in this early photograph still stand today, confronting the very different scene generated by the frenetic age of the motor vehicle.

By the 1920s the motor car was making its mark. This one is about to turn into Market Street from Teme Street at Gardner's Corner, named after the 'Central Bazaar' of A.E. Gardner which at that time occupied the corner premises.

This imposing arch, giving every impression of leading to an ancient abbey, was in fact the entrance to Tenbury's Corn Exchange. Since 1954 when this picture was taken, the arch has disappeared and the Corn Exchange site is now occupied by the firm Bedford Dials.

By the 1950s Teme Street was beginning to take on an appearance a little nearer that of today, but as yet there were no obtrusive yellow lines to thwart parking. The Court, seen at the end of the street, was still a few years away from its demolition.

This early photograph shows the yard behind the seventeenth-century Ship Inn in Teme Street. There was once provision here to accommodate a hundred horses. Nowadays it's all part of a pleasant patio and garden area for customers.

The Crow Hotel is another of Tenbury's seventeenth-century hostelries. Once boasting extensive stabling, it was considerably altered by the Victorians.

The yard behind the Crow Hotel in 1920 was not one of the town's more salubrious locations. This scene has now long disappeared to become a car-park for the patrons of today.

A turn-of-the-century view of the bridge over the little Kyre Brook, with part of the Crow Hotel on the left. Through the trees in the background can be glimpsed the Pump Room which was built in 1862 following the discovery of mineral springs in 1839.

A closer view of the Pump Room from the Kyre Bridge, showing the ornamental gardens in which it was once set. The Victorian extensions to the Crow Hotel, just seen on the left, were in anticipation of the crowds of cure-seekers who were expected to descend on the town.

Metal-clad and built in an extraordinary style described as 'Chinese Gothic', the Pump Room was distinguished by this prominent pagoda, nowadays in an advanced state of decay.

A general view of the Pump Room when it was still relatively new. The building contained men's and women's bathrooms, and consulting rooms in which rheumatic and arthritic visitors could discuss their ailments with the spa doctors.

Tenbury's spa water could either be bathed in or drunk. The early bath seen here, complete with four taps, was originally installed in the Pump Room but is now in the town's museum. Next to it is an ornate drinking fountain, also from the Pump Room.

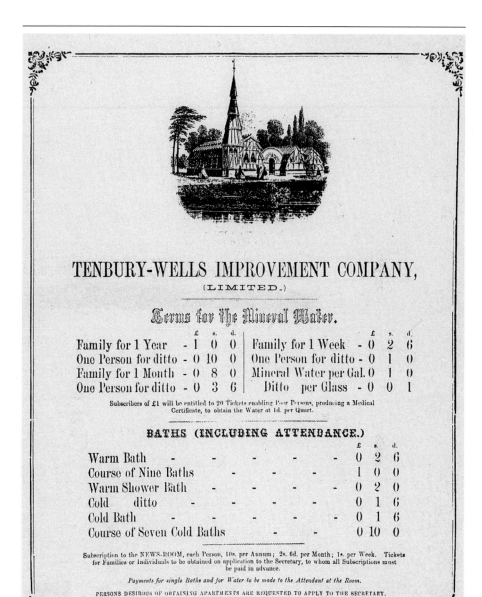

TENBURY-WELLS IMPROVEMENT COMPANY,
(LIMITED.)

Terms for the Mineral Water.

	£	s.	d.		£	s.	d.
Family for 1 Year -	1	0	0	Family for 1 Week -	0	2	6
One Person for ditto -	0	10	0	One Person for ditto -	0	1	0
Family for 1 Month -	0	8	0	Mineral Water per Gal.	0	1	0
One Person for ditto -	0	3	6	Ditto per Glass -	0	0	1

Subscribers of £1 will be entitled to 20 Tickets enabling Poor Persons, producing a Medical Certificate, to obtain the Water at 1d. per Quart.

BATHS (INCLUDING ATTENDANCE.)

	£	s.	d.
Warm Bath - - - - -	0	2	6
Course of Nine Baths - - -	1	0	0
Warm Shower Bath - - - -	0	2	0
Cold ditto - - - -	0	1	6
Cold Bath - - - - -	0	1	6
Course of Seven Cold Baths - -	0	10	0

Subscription to the NEWS-ROOM, each Person, 10s. per Annum; 2s. 6d. per Month; 1s. per Week. Tickets for Families or Individuals to be obtained on application to the Secretary, to whom all Subscriptions must be paid in advance.

Payments for single Baths and for Water to be made to the Attendant at the Room.

PERSONS DESIROUS OF OBTAINING APARTMENTS ARE REQUESTED TO APPLY TO THE SECRETARY.

[*By Order*] ROBERT ROBINSON, *Secretary.*

Tenbury, 1863.

R. HOME, PRINTER, TENBURY-WELLS.

Dated 1863, this tariff of charges was displayed by the Tenbury Wells Improvement Company which operated the Pump Room. A warm therapeutic shower bath could be had for 2s, or you could drink a glass of mineral water for 1d.

The Court, by the side of the Kyre Brook, once dominated the southern end of Teme Street. Formerly the home of the Godson family, the building stood in spacious grounds, which included these tennis courts, but was demolished in the 1960s to make way for a modern housing development.

In its day The Court was a handsome mansion, and the original house on the site was believed to have been moated. Much of the building which survived to the 1960s dated from the eighteenth century and was extended in about 1850.

The bridge over the Kyre Brook at the beginning of the twentieth century. On the right is part of the Crow Hotel and in the background a glimpse of Market Street. The building above the bridge in the centre of the picture is on the site of an early market hall. From this point the waters of the Kyre Brook flow behind the east side of Teme Street to join the Teme at Dorothy's Rock. The spot is so called because a woman named Dorothy is said to have slipped into the river on her way home one dark night and was drowned.

Market Street, from its junction with Teme Street, as it looked about a century ago. The impressive store on the right was at that time occupied by Wheeler's, whose name still appears on the doorstep. The premises have since been converted into individual shops.

Another early view of Market Street. With only one horse-drawn wagon in sight, the street presents a very different picture from the busy traffic-filled thoroughfare of today.

Market Street, 1892. Pre-eminent among the buildings in Market Street is the Royal Oak, with its eye-catching frontage of decorative timbering. Although generally accepted as being largely Jacobean in origin, it could be even older. Like other Royal Oak hostelries up and down the country, its name is derived from the oak tree in which Charles II hid during his dramatic escape after the Battle of Worcester. The shop to the left of the inn has now given way to a parking space.

A leisurely scene of Victorian shoppers going about their daily business in Market Street.

Victorian Market Street again. Sam Mattock, landlord of the Royal Oak, evidently felt his name should be given equal prominence to that of his inn. He was formerly Tenbury's station master.

Arguably, Tenbury's best-known secular building is the Round Market, an apparent misnomer as the building is oval. It was built in 1862 on the site of an earlier covered market.

Facing the Round Market in Market Square is the handsome frontage of Holland House, seen here in use by Lloyds Bank before the bank opened its present branch in Teme Street. Today the building is subdivided into solicitors' offices and a private residence.

This row of timbered cottages once graced Church Street until they were demolished to make room for a modern bungalow. Church Street was the main thoroughfare through the town, until Teme Street became the principal trading street when the medieval bridge was built.

Another view of the cottages pictured above. Judging by the dress of the three ladies, the photograph was taken early this century. The two-storey brick house just beyond the cottages has been rebuilt further back to make room for a new development called Scotland Place.

A view of the parish church of St Mary seen across the River Teme in 1892. Although the origins of the church can be traced back to Norman times, much of the present building is Victorian. A large part of the church was destroyed in the great flood of 1770, and although it was repaired in 1777, a major rebuilding took place in 1864. Part of the original Norman tower survived not only the 1770 flood but both the subsequent restorations, and still stands today as evidence of the church's deep roots in history.

The interior of St Mary's Church before the removal of the rood screen between the chancel and nave earlier this century. The previous restoration work of 1864 had been carried out by the eminent Victorian architect Henry Woodyer.

Another interior view of the church after the rood screen had been removed. The pulpit had been changed earlier, and the Lady Chapel was refurbished and given a memorial window to a long-serving church warden who died in 1904, William Norris.

An early photograph of the parish church from Church Street. During the 1864 restoration part of a Saxon preaching cross from around AD 880 was discovered, and it is now preserved as one of the church's numerous ecclesiastical and historical treasures. A waist-high flood-mark plaque by the chancel arch is a stark reminder of the depth of water which invaded the church on 14 May 1886. The little building seen here on the left of the churchyard entrance has seen a varied existence, first as a mortuary, then as a fire station and meeting room.

Seventeenth-century Cornwall House in Cross Street with its Dutch-style gables. Built as a dower house for the Cornwall family of Burford Castle, it is said, according to local legend, to be linked to the parish church by a tunnel.

A neighbour of Cornwall House is the seventeenth-century half-timbered King's Head, another notable survivor of the many inns which Tenbury could once boast. It seems here to be receiving a delivery from the Great Western Railway, one of whose lorries is parked outside.

Another view of Cross Street looking towards the town centre. The sight of a photographer in Victorian Tenbury was obviously one not to be missed, certainly not by these schoolchildren who were probably pupils at Goff's Free School which is tucked away between the buildings on the right. The original school was founded in 1816 but the present building, which was once used as a Baptist chapel, bears the date 1863 on its porch and now serves as Tenbury Museum.

A reminder of the southern end of Cross Street when it was little more than a country lane. The timbered building on the left is sixteenth-century Pembroke House, a former farmhouse which became an inn. It still exists as possibly the oldest public house in Tenbury.

A closer view of Mount Lodge, or Mount Cottage, seen in the background of the top picture. On the corner of the road to Bromyard, it was originally the lodge to the nearby house called The Mount, and possibly once served as a tollhouse.

After its use as a farmhouse, Pembroke House became a cider house selling a particularly potent rough cider made in Tenbury. In the 1930s its preference switched to beer and it changed its role to that of a more conventional public house.

These old cottages once stood in what was known as Trumpet Yard off Cross Street. They were demolished to make way for the modern Pembroke Gardens housing development for the elderly.

Once overlooking quaintly named Bog Lane, picturesque Pound Cottage has now disappeared. The town pound was originally located nearby.

If fate dealt an unkind blow to Pound Cottage (pictured top), it has treated Greenhill Cottage more agreeably. This attractive little dwelling, now much altered, still exists by the side of the Kyre Brook. The small child is John Phillips who became a well-known Tenbury barber.

The Capricious Teme

Throughout all the centuries of Tenbury's existence, the River Teme on which the town stands, has proved both friend and enemy. Loved for its beauty and for the matchless character it bestows on the valley through which it flows, it is also feared in times of flood. On countless occasions, when its waters have been swollen by the rains of the Welsh hills at its source and by its many tributaries, the river has burst its banks with dramatic effect, inundating Tenbury and the surrounding countryside. Nowadays, with the help of modern technology, remedial measures have been taken to minimise the likelihood of further severe flooding on the scale the town has known in the past. But the Teme's behaviour has always been unpredictable, and who knows when it will once again be moved to unleash its floodwaters on a town which has had to brave the consequences all too often? In the pages that follow are some graphic reminders of Tenbury under water.

At 9 a.m. on an autumn morning in 1946, after a period of incessant rain, this was the scene which greeted the people of Tenbury. The river had risen to the top of the arches of the bridge, and was already bursting its banks.

In 1947 one of the worst floods this century occurred. This photograph shows the river almost up to the level of the roadway on the bridge, and still rising.

The scene downstream from Tenbury Bridge during the 1947 floods. Already several times its normal width, the river resembles a vast lake. The gas-holders on the left have long been dismantled.

After the 1947 floods had begun to subside this was the scene at Tenbury Bridge. The pressure of debris against the structure would have been tremendous, and it is little wonder that before it was strengthened the bridge was frequently damaged in times of flood.

This picture of the 1947 floods shows the Castle Tump (centre background) islanded by the Teme. There is a theory that at one time the river actually flowed past the Tump before severe flooding diverted its course.

In the 1946 floods this was the scene along the riverside footpath leading from the bridge to the Burgage Recreation Ground which lies behind the eastern side of Teme Street.

A lonely horse tethered at the roadside is one of the few signs of life in this photograph of flooded Teme Street, taken from Gardner's Corner around the turn of the century. This is a scene which at one time was all too familiar to Tenbury shopkeepers. Even this disastrous inundation was mild compared with what has become known as the Great Flood of 1770, when the force of the water demolished much of the parish church.

Berrington Road, which runs parallel to the Teme to the west of the town, was easy prey for the swollen river in the floods of 1946, and took on the appearance of a canal. One intrepid Tenburian appears to be pitting his wits against the rising water.

Flooded Market Street about a century ago. Until the water subsided, there was little anyone could do but stand and stare. The shop called Hole in the Wall still exists today as a health food store.

The year was 1900 and the Teme had again broken its banks, a sight which evidently fascinated this crowd of onlookers. The building behind the lamppost has now been extended and is occupied by Lloyds Bank.

Market Street in flood during the 1920s. Fortunately for this lone car driver the water was shallow enough for him to make his journey.

Harry Higgins stands outside his waterlogged ironmongery and hardware shop in Teme Street during the 1947 flood. He had the distinction of being the only person to have swum the whole length of flooded Teme Street on two occasions.

Floodwater is no respecter of boundaries or property. This was the scene early this century in an unidentified part of the town, believed to be near the yard off Cross Street now occupied by Caldicott's, the building contractors.

Floods or no floods, the milk had to be delivered. When this 1947 picture was taken, the Second World War had been over for less than two years, and the wartime spirit of perseverance obviously persisted for Mr Archer Booton and Mr John Griffiths.

Teme Street looking towards the bridge during the floods of 1947. This is a scene more reminiscent of Venice than Tenbury Wells.

This is the opposite view to the one above, looking up Teme Street from outside the council offices. The main road leading from the bridge is on the other side of the railings on the right.

Market Street with its shops boarded up looked a sorry sight during the floods of 1947. The floods in this part of the town were swollen by the waters of the Kyre Brook which flows parallel to the street just out of view to the left.

Local historian Eric Lowe surveys the 1947 floods at the junction of Market Street and Teme Street. It was his collection of memorabilia, amassed later during the 1970s, which formed the nucleus of Tenbury's present-day museum. Note the nostalgic sign to Tenbury's now long-gone station.

Where there's a will there's a way. For one adventurous citizen, Robin Phillips, the best way to navigate flooded Market Street in 1947 was by canoe.

A boat was also the answer in the 1910 floods. Here, Mr Gerald Godson is rowed by his groom from Market Street into Teme Street. The Godsons, who lived at The Court, were an influential local family, regarded by many as the Squires of Tenbury.

Where do we go from here? A group of townsfolk regard the floods from the bridge approach early this century. Beyond is Teme Street, with the Bridge Hotel on the right. In his history of Tenbury, published in 1931, the Reverend Wayland Joyce, a former Rector of Burford, wrote: 'Tenbury has suffered again and again very severely from floods. A big flood there is an alarming event when it comes. Perhaps the after effects are still more serious, through the damp, the smells, and the consequent disease which follow the flooding of the cellars and drains. . . .'

Even flooding as severe as that in 1947 failed to dampen the enthusiasm of this group of regulars at the Royal Oak in Market Street. They seem to be in good spirits as they gather at the pub's entrance.

Another view of one of Market Street's many inundations. The building in the foreground, known as the Clock House, still exists as shop premises, but the small building between it and the Royal Oak is no longer there.

Roll out the barrel. Having presumably escaped from the cellars of a public house, these barrels are floating away across the Market Square in a flood during the 1920s.

A council lorry comes to the aid of a stricken bus during the 1947 floods. During severe flooding such as this, the disruption to normal life in Tenbury was immense.

The aftermath of a typical Tenbury flood. The damage to property caused by water and mud was often incalculable, and shop owners in particular were badly hit. Sandbags were only of limited use and there was nothing for it but to wait until the water receded and then clear up the mess, as this hard-working group is trying to do. Mud was not only confined to the streets. It was all-pervasive, covering cellars and ground floors and leaving behind an obnoxious smell which often took a long time to disperse.

Workaday Tenbury

Tenbury is a market town in the true sense of the word. As early as 1249, King Henry III granted a charter to the town enabling it to hold regular markets, and the custom has flourished ever since. The weekly produce and livestock markets are still a cherished feature of local life. Despite its modest size, Tenbury has always been an important regional commercial centre, and its shops, as well as its markets, serve a wide rural area. The heyday of the hopyards and orchards may now belong to the past, but they continue to make a contribution to the local economy, while farming still flourishes as a traditional staple industry in the Teme Valley. And in the spirit of twentieth-century economic diversification, Tenbury can even boast its own industrial and trading estates, and a mini business park. In the following pages are reminders of some of the ways in which the local people spent their working days in earlier times.

A typical livestock market day in years gone by. Tenbury's traditional markets, both livestock and produce, are still highspots in the local calendar and attract buyers and sellers from a wide surrounding area.

Mechanization and modern practices may have reduced the number of people working on the land since this 1908 picture was taken, but farming is still widespread in the Teme Valley. This shallow stretch of river near Tenbury Bridge gave one farmer a welcome opportunity to water his cattle.

Hop-pickers of long ago hard at work in one of the local hopyards. Even the little child on the right appears to be joining in with enthusiasm. At one time hop-growing was a major occupation in the borderlands of Worcestershire, Shropshire and Herefordshire, and is mentioned in records dating back as far as the early 1400s when hops were described as a 'wicked weed'. Nowadays, although hopyards can still be seen around Tenbury, their number has diminished dramatically.

Hop-picking towards the end of the last century. Whole families were often hired to help with the vital task of harvesting, usually in September.

Victorian hop-pickers set to work in a hopyard near Tenbury. The importance of anticipating the success of a crop is reflected in this old local adage: 'Till St James's Day be come and gone, there may be hops or there may be none.' St James's Day is on 25 July.

In a region as famous for its apple orchards as its hops, it is not surprising that cider making – and cider drinking – were once important local activities. This early photograph recalls the custom of taking all the necessary apparatus into the orchards, and actually producing cider on the spot.

Haymakers working for the Godson family who lived at The Court and whose many local interests included farming.

Not surprisingly, the production of hop poles was once an essential local occupation. This early picture shows two wagon loads of poles passing Pembroke House.

This Victorian photograph shows the little stationer's shop run by S. Barwise which once stood next to the Royal Oak in Market Street. It has now disappeared and in its place is a space for parking cars.

Another Victorian photograph showing a corner of Tenbury which has since changed. The view is towards the Market Square from Cross Street, before the old shops on the left were demolished.

The Market Square, with the Round Market at its heart, has always been a busy scene on market days. This picture, taken in the early years of this century, shows traders arriving with their produce in a variety of hand-carts and horse-drawn wagons.

Another view of the same bustling scene captured in the top picture. It is to be hoped that the young boy crossing the road on the left spotted the oncoming horse and cart in time.

More market day activity in days gone by. The original charter to hold a market, requested by local landowner Roger de Clifford and granted by Henry III, is preserved to this day among the records of the Master of the Rolls in the Tower of London. It begins: 'Know ye that we have granted and by this our Charter confirmed for us and our heirs to our beloved and faithful Roger de Clifford, that he and his heirs may have for ever one Market every week on Tuesday at his Manor of Temetebury. . . .' Note the early spelling of Tenbury.

Apart from the trading carried on inside the Round Market, stalls were set up along the roadside in the Market Square. This early photograph shows them being prepared for the day's business.

Trading gets under way as the public arrives. Note the crowd in the background. As is still the case today, people from many of the surrounding villages support Tenbury's market. The Market Hotel on the left is now the Market Tavern.

The traditional hustle and bustle of market day is again well captured in this photograph taken about the time of the First World War. Note the number of people looking at the camera, a relatively rare experience in those days.

A slightly more recent photograph of the same scenes depicted above and on the opposite page. Note the height of the tree above the rooftop in the background. In the lower picture opposite, it is just peeping above the same building.

Judging by the number of butchers' shops which once served Tenbury, the local people must have been avid meat eaters. This shop in the Market Square was evidently preparing for Christmas, as the baskets in the foreground contain holly and mistletoe.

A closer view of the shop in the top picture, complete with the butcher's smart delivery cart. By today's standards, the boy in the apron seems young to be serving in a shop.

This splendid photograph of the premises of Burch the butcher was taken at Christmas in 1895, and the staff seem delighted to pose for a picture. Considering this was not the only butcher in the town at that time, they were obviously expecting to sell an enormous amount of meat over the Christmas period. The question of food safety and hygiene was evidently not a priority in Victorian Tenbury. If a butcher today displayed his meat in this fashion, he would be closed without argument.

This well-stocked shop is believed to have been at the corner of Cross Street and Berrington Road. If so, the building still exists, although much altered, and now serves as an Indian restaurant.

Such was the amount and variety of meat on display at this Teme Street shop, that the butcher, like the one in the top picture, resorted to a kerbside table to gain extra space.

This butcher's shop in the Market Square was owned by the Bowkett family which is still in business in Tenbury today with a modern food store and a wholesale butcher's depot. As in the other early photographs of butchers' shops, the staff are out in force to pose for the camera. With all that meat hanging from the building and stacked on the pavement, it's tempting to wonder what was in the dog's mind.

This bicycle shop in Teme Street was owned by T.H. Wyile who was in the trade for over fifty years. The photograph was taken shortly before the First World War.

A trio of smithies at the old forge in Cross Street which once occupied the little gabled building in the left foreground of the picture on page 67. This is now used as a veterinary surgery.

Shoes in abundant variety decorate the frontage of Dancer's shoe shop which once traded in Teme Street. The shop still exists, but sells greengrocery rather than shoes.

Until the advent of the motor car, the saddler and harness-maker was a necessity in any town. This well-stocked shop in Teme Street later became a branch of Barclays Bank (see picture on page 76).

The small two-storey building in this early photograph of Teme Street was the Tenbury branch of Barclays Bank before the bank moved into its present larger premises between the wars.

Another of Tenbury's early saddlery businesses, with the wife of the proprietor, Mrs Gore, standing in the doorway. Like the saddlery shop pictured on the previous page, it was situated in Teme Street.

Long gone are the days when you could buy a new jacket for 5s, or 25p, like those being displayed by Frank J. Bloom in his Teme Street clothing shop in the early years of the century. The art of window dressing had yet to make its mark on Tenbury's shops, and it was quite customary for as much as possible to be packed into every available space in order to attract the attention of passers-by. These premises still exist, now subdivided between an optometrist and the local office of the National Farmers' Union.

Sheltering from the rain outside the Clock House, so named because of its clock which still looks out over Market Street. This 1950s photograph shows the building in use as a corn store. It still exists, now much altered, selling meat, provisions and greengrocery.

Charlie Woodward sits in his Austin Seven outside his garden shop in Cross Street. The building is still occupied by a similar business, Teme Valley Nurseries.

An early group photograph of the staff at Tenbury's post office. This was before the arrival of motor vehicles, so the resident horse has been persuaded to appear in the picture too.

The post office staff again, in a picture taken about the same time as the one above. The post office building itself is still used for the same purpose today.

Watering the streets was a regular and necessary activity in years gone by, before the advent of mechanical street-cleansing vehicles. Receiving attention here is Church Street.

The traction engine, now more likely to be seen at fairs and rallies, was once a common sight in Tenbury. This handsome vehicle is parked outside the Swan Hotel with wagons loaded with stone from the quarries on Clee Hill.

Tracks to Tenbury

When Dr Beeching wielded his axe on Britain's railway network in the 1960s the line serving Tenbury was one of the casualties. It had opened about a hundred years earlier, replacing the ill-fated Kington, Leominster and Stourport Canal which, although serving Tenbury, never progressed much further east than Newnham. The railway line, operated by the GWR, linked up with the main Shrewsbury to Hereford line at Woofferton Junction, and with the Bridgnorth to Kidderminster line at Bewdley. Parts of its original track can still be discerned and several of its buildings and bridges survive. But Tenbury station has given way to an industrial estate, and the days when the whistle of a chuffing steam train could be heard echoing across the Teme Valley are now nothing but a nostalgic memory for those old enough to remember. The pictures in the following pages recall some of the sights from those far-off days.

Tenbury Wells station in 1908. The photographer had obviously persuaded the staff to space themselves along the platform to give added interest.

The Tenbury junction on the main Shrewsbury to Hereford line was at Woofferton, seen here with one of the Tenbury line tank engines at the platform.

A general view of Tenbury station early this century. It was actually sited a short distance from the town at Burford, after local landowner Lord Northwick had joined with others to campaign for the line to be built. Apart from its two platforms, the station boasted cattle pens, goods sidings and, in its early years, a turntable. Initially it also had two signal boxes, but one was closed in the 1920s.

Captured on film for posterity was this accident at Tenbury station early this century. The crane had been vainly attempting to lift this giant tree trunk in the goods yard, when it toppled over. The four workmen do not seem particularly perturbed.

Fencing work on one of the station platforms. Unfortunately, records do not confirm whether the fence was being built, dismantled or merely repaired.

In 1913 a number of alterations took place at Tenbury station, and to celebrate the fact the staff posed for a group photograph. For the station master, identified as Mr Roberts (middle, front row), an armchair evidently befitted his rank. Also in the picture is signalman Dick Jay (third from left, centre row), and Fred Jones, the station's horse-dray driver (fifth from left, centre row).

One of Tenbury's most memorable characters was Reg Mytton, whose eccentricities involved him in many local affairs. Here he is on Tenbury station, suitably attired for the occasion, awaiting the very last train in the early 1960s.

A nostalgic reminder of the last passenger train to leave Tenbury station for Woofferton Junction in 1961.

A general view of Tenbury looking over the railway goods sidings in 1918, long before they succumbed to Dr Beeching's axe. The section of the line to Woofferton Junction closed to passengers on 31 July 1961, and the section to Bewdley on 1 August 1962. The station remained open to freight traffic until January 1964 when it finally closed for good.

An early reminder of the lane leading to Tenbury station. In the foreground is the Rose & Crown inn which is still here, although now fronted by a car-park rather than a fence and hedge.

This early horse-drawn carriage, affectionately known as the Tenbury Bus, was employed to ferry railway passengers to and from the Swan Hotel which is pictured here.

Waiting in Tenbury station in the early 1960s is one of the GWR's diesel railcars which supplemented steam services on branch lines in many parts of the country. This was one of the last diesel railcars to use the line before closure. The name-board on the far platform is a reminder that the station was orginally known as just plain Tenbury. In 1912 it was renamed Tenbury Wells presumably in recognition of the town's efforts to establish itself as a spa.

This photograph, taken shortly after the Second World War, shows the station and goods sidings still in use. The Rose & Crown (also pictured on page 88) can be seen by the station approach road near the bottom left-hand corner. Further along the same road, the line of tractors and trailers is queuing to deliver fruit from the local orchards to a cider and perry manufacturer on the industrial estate. Since the railway closed, the estate has expanded to engulf the whole station site.

Tenburians

Depicted in some of the photographs in earlier pages have been a few of the people who, in a variety of ways, have contributed to the fabric of day-to-day life in the town in years gone by. In the section which follows, there are glimpses of others, young and old, who have likewise played their part in the Tenbury story.

Tenbury's football club early this century. The left-hand player in the back row is the young Harry Higgins, who is pictured later in life on page 50 outside his ironmongery shop. The town still has a thriving football club.

The town has always supported a wide variety of clubs and societies to cater for the many interests of the local people. This is the Tenbury Gun Club posing for a photograph in 1909.

Tenbury Bowling Club, founded in 1894, is another longstanding institution still flourishing today. Its first president was a distinguished local solicitor, William Norris, who was the churchwarden commemorated by a window in the parish church (see page 36). The first captain was Sam Mattock, licensee at the Royal Oak. This photograph shows the club members in about 1900.

Boys attending the National School, or 'Top School' as it became known, pose for a photograph with their teachers towards the end of the last century. Mr Rees, the headmaster, is on the left.

Another group of 'Top School' pupils, this time photographed in the girls' playground. On the left is Tom Long, the then headmaster.

An old English rural tradition rarely seen today. Watched by a large crowd of onlookers, local children demonstrate the art of maypole dancing.

Choosing a May Queen was another custom enjoyed by local children. In this pre-1918 photograph, the proud winner wears her garland as she poses with her attendants in their spotless white dresses.

A 1909 photograph of the original National School. The building is now a residential education centre known as More House, run by St Thomas More School at Willenhall in the West Midlands. Today the town is served by its C. of E. Primary School and Tenbury High School.

On the edge of Tenbury stands the impressive Victorian church of St Michael, connected to St Michael's College which formerly housed one of England's leading choir schools.

Pupils of St Michael's College at dinner in 1955. The college ceased to be a boys' choir school in 1985 and is now owned by King's College, Madrid. The college and the adjacent church were founded in 1856 by the eminent church musician, Sir Frederick Gore Ouseley.

Photographed with his donkey around the turn of the century, was this colourful Tenbury character affectionately known throughout the town as Donkey Davis. He carried local produce between Tenbury and Rochford for many years.

Lord Northwick photographed towards the end of the last century. Although his family seat was at Northwick Park in Gloucestershire, he was an influential landowner in the Tenbury area. Among his family's possessions was the Burford estate.

During the First World War, the members of Tenbury Music Society gave numerous concert parties, not only in the town but in many of the surrounding villages. In this photograph taken in 1916, they are about to set off on just such a mission. This is an interesting study of the fashions of the day when it was customary for most people never to be seen out of doors without wearing a hat.

The vicar of Tenbury, the Revd Murray Ragg, addresses an unidentified gathering on the lawns of The Court. This was the home of 'Squire' Gerald Godson, seen here impeccably dressed in his white flannels and boater. The year was 1920.

Like the photograph on page 99, this is another interesting study of the fashions of the period – in this case the 1920s. The occasion was a wedding reception at the Ship Hotel.

With Church Street in the background, the Market Square provides the setting for a hunt meet in 1907, probably the Ludlow Hounds.

Not surprisingly, the sight of elephants disporting themselves in the Teme drew large crowds to the bridge in 1905. The creatures would have been part of Wombwell's Menagerie which made regular visits to Tenbury from 1874 onwards.

This early 1970s photograph is interesting on two counts. It depicts one of Tenbury's most popular activities, the weekly Women's Institute market, and it shows the interior of the old Pump Room before the building had reached its present state of dilapidation. The unusual pointed windows relate to the building's extraordinary Chinese style of architecture, described in Section One.

SECTION SIX

War and Peace

Some of the ways in which Tenbury was involved with the army in both war and peace captured the imagination of local photographers in the early years of the present century, and a selection of their pictures appears in the following pages. There are glimpses, too, of the civil powers – the fire brigade and the police – who served the town and its environs in years gone by.

Tenbury Town Band joined with the local Territorials for this photograph outside the Pump Room shortly before the First World War.

Soon after this group photograph of local Territorials was taken, the First World War began and the men found themselves on active service.

A contingent of local soldiers marches to Tenbury railway station at the outbreak of the First World War. It appears that many of the town's youngsters would have liked to join them.

The troops in the top picture were not obliged to carry their baggage while they marched to the station. This followed in horse-drawn carts, suitably guarded by foot soldiers with rifles.

One of the most poignant episodes for the people of Tenbury at the outbreak of the First World War was the impressment of horses. Owners were obliged to hand over their animals to the military authorities, almost certain that they would never see them again.

The documentation connected with the impressment of horses for the war meant a long queue for these Tenbury owners. The soldier on duty seems more interested in the camera than in overseeing the proceedings.

On 5 August 1914, one officer and forty-four other ranks of 'B' Company, 7th Battalion, the Worcestershire Regiment wait on Tenbury station for a train to Kidderminster as they set off for the war. This was a scene repeated all over the country as final preparations were made for what was sincerely, if naïvely, regarded as 'the war to end all wars'.

In 1913 these Territorials, in their ceremonial uniforms, were photographed marching through Tenbury for a church parade at the parish church. A year later they were to be drafted for active service.

Police Inspector Milsom (seated centre) served at Tenbury in the early years of the century, but it appears he never had his photograph taken while working in the town. This picture is believed to have been taken in Redditch to where he was later posted.

The men of Tenbury's fire brigade oblige the photographer by posing outside the parish church with their horse-drawn and manual appliances.

Members of the fire brigade in action. Whether this was an exercise or a real fire is not recorded. The smiling fireman second from right, is Bill Hartland, one of the town's blacksmiths.

Moving their cumbersome appliance could often be an arduous task for local firemen when a fire was some distance from a road. Here, members of the public lend a willing hand.

On 22 October 1914 a barn fire occurred at Sutton House off the Bromyard road. The Tenbury brigade was summoned to deal with it, and photographed in action.

It was a proud day when the Tenbury brigade took delivery of a new motor fire engine. Aboard are Captain G.E.T.H. Maund and Deputy Captain Howells. Other well-known local names among the crew include Holden, Keeley, Hartland, Lloyd and Bob Jones.

Before the present modern fire station was built on the Worcester road, appliances were kept in part of the council offices in Teme Street, seen here. This fire engine is of less ancient vintage than the machine pictured at the top.

One of the stalwarts of Tenbury's fire brigade early this century was Deputy Captain Howells who looks an imposing sight in the smart uniform of the day.

Deputy Captain Howells' daughter Minnie proudly poses with her doll outside a door bearing her father's title. After her marriage she became Mrs Minnie Williams.

Round About

The countryside around Tenbury is richly varied, from the ruggedness of the Shropshire hills to the undulating farmland of Worcestershire and Herefordshire, with the lushness of the Teme Valley providing a unifying link. Dotted about within a radius of just a few miles of Tenbury, is a wealth of hamlets and villages of no less varied character, and in the selection of early photographs in the following pages, there are glimpses of just a small cross-section. Some depict scenes within these communities in years gone by, often very little changed from the same scenes today. Others recall aspects of local life which now belong firmly in the pages of history. Collectively, as with the pictures of Tenbury itself in earlier sections, they provide a valuable historical record as well as a visual acknowledgement of the efforts of many an unknown photographer.

At Oldwood Common, straddling the main Leominster road to the south of Tenbury, this diminutive chapel once served the Primitive Methodists who have gathered in force for this early photograph.

Around the turn of the century, the temperance movement was constantly warning against the perceived evils of the demon drink. Judging by the appearance of the Oldwood Temperance Band, music was a useful weapon in the campaigners' armoury.

A nostalgic reminder of the days when the Tenbury to Bewdley railway line served the village of Neen Sollars is this early photograph of the picturesque Railway Tavern. The course of the old railway has now been largely reclaimed by nature, but the inn still survives, and for old time's sake its sign depicts a splendid picture of an early steam locomotive.

Another delightful picture which reflects the formal fashions popular around the turn of the century. The occasion was the wedding of Mr Artie Maund and Miss Annie Mees at Knighton-on-Teme.

The Victorian church of St Lawrence in the Teme Valley hamlet of Lindridge provides the background for this 1908 wedding scene. The fine old car would have been something of a modern phenomenon in rural Worcestershire at that time.

The eighteenth-century bridge at Eastham spans the Teme a few miles downstream from Tenbury. This picture is taken from an early watercolour showing the tollhouse which at one time stood next to the bridge.

A 1920s photograph of the Teme, looking through one of the arches of Eastham Bridge. Not far away stands the Norman church of St Peter and St Paul, one of Worcestershire's most interesting early rural churches.

A reminder of the heyday of the Woofferton Junction to Tenbury railway line before it closed in the 1960s. This is the little country station known grandly as 'Easton Court for Little Hereford' a few miles to the west of Tenbury. Today, still recognizable, it serves as a private house.

This idyllic 1920s scene at Little Hereford has remained unaltered over the years. The footbridge still spans the Teme, tucked away behind the parish church which is hidden behind the trees.

A diesel railcar waits at Newnham Bridge in 1961, shortly before the Tenbury line closed. This archetypal country station has now been partially restored and serves as a garden centre and shop.

The Talbot Hotel, seen here before the Second World War, still stands near the site of Newnham Bridge station at the point where the Tenbury road joins the main roads to Kidderminster and Worcester. It is an impressive example of the Victorians' penchant for Gothic-style architecture.

Early in the present century, this old forge was still serving the many needs of the village of Boraston, just to the north-east of Tenbury. It still exists, now transformed into an attractive private bungalow.

To the north of Tenbury lies the village of Cleehill, on the edge of the Shropshire hill which shares its name. This early picture was taken nearby at Cornbrook Bridge. The peaceful road is just recognizable as the modern A4117 as it climbs over Clee between Ludlow and Kidderminster.

Towards the end of the last century, a serious landslip occurred at Aston Bank close to the village of Boraston. Watched by a group of onlookers, the repair work stopped for a moment while the workmen posed for this picture.

The little Norman church of St Michael in its timeless setting by the Teme at Rochford. This between-the-wars picture could be duplicated today with few changes being detectable.

The grounds, lake and church at Kyre Park, off the Tenbury to Bromyard road, provide a splendid setting for this social gathering early this century. The mansion, which has been both a wartime convalescent home and a centre for spastics, is now a private residence.

A late-Victorian scene near Kyrewood on the outskirts of Tenbury, as workers make their way to help with the hop or fruit harvest.

A century or more ago Mr William Smith of Kyre Green near Tenbury evidently grew a bumper crop of swedes, according to this early advertising photograph. The placard announces that the yield of 40 tons per acre was accomplished with the help of 'Hadfield's No. 1 Turnip Manure'.

A rural scene by the Greete Brook not far from Tenbury. Since this early photograph was taken, the bridge and footpath have become largely obscured by undergrowth, although they still exist.

A misty view over Burford and Tenbury captured by a photographer in 1892 from the road leading to the neighbouring hamlet of Greete.

The former Bell Inn at Broad Heath, not to be confused with Broadheath near Worcester where Elgar was born. The inn, now restored and boasting a large car-park, is known today as the Tally Ho.

The Teme at Stanford Bridge on the road from Great Witley to Bromyard. The picture was taken soon after the graceful single-arch structure was built in 1905. It has since been superseded by a modern replacement.

Meadows Mill by the Teme at Eardiston, with its eel trap (left) and mill wheel. Its working days long passed, the old mill now serves as an attractive holiday cottage.

An early delivery van waits outside the Nag's Head Inn which, now extended and smartly refurbished, still guards the junction of the main Tenbury to Great Witley road with the lane to the village of Frith Common.

A late-Victorian view of Brimfield which has long passed into the pages of history. Occupying the site of these old cottages today is the village post office and a car-park for the local inn, The Roebuck.

In 1947, the flooded Teme engulfed the grounds of Burford House, built in 1728 on the site of Burford Castle, ancient home of the Cornwall family. The magnificent gardens, created by the late Mr John Treasure, are open to the public, and the adjacent nursery and garden centre, known nationwide as Treasures of Tenbury, contains the National Clematis Collection.

Acknowledgements

For the willing help and advice given to the compiler during his researches, grateful acknowledgement is made to the following: Betty Boffey, who kindly allowed access to her late husband's photographic collection; John Bright, and Neville Bright, chairman of the Tenbury & District Museum Society, for permission to use pictures from their collections; and Howard Miller, secretary of the Tenbury Wells and District Civic and Historical Society, for his help in supplying photographs and other historical material. Acknowledgement is also made to the following for kindly allowing the reproduction of specific pictures: David Kendrick for the picture (page 21) taken by his late father, Mr G.R. Kendrick; the Hereford & Worcester County Record Office (page 23, lower); the Frith Collection, Shaftesbury, Dorset, for the pictures on pages 16 (lower), 22 (upper), 119 (lower), 120 (lower); *Birmingham Post & Mail* (page 97); *Worcester Evening News* (page 102). Although considerable effort has been made to trace the owners of all the illustrations reproduced in these pages, this has not proved possible in every case. To those who have remained elusive, the compiler and publishers offer grateful acknowledgement for any of their pictures which are included.